Totline "Take-Home" Books

Animal Rhymes

Reproducible Pre-Reading Books
For Young Children

Written by Jean Warren • Illustrated by Judith Prowse Buskirk

Editorial Staff: Gayle Bittinger, Elizabeth McKinnon, Susan M. Sexton, Jean Warren
Production Director: Eileen Carbary
Design: Kathy Jones
Cover-Computer Graphics: Eric Stovall
Inside Pages-Text and Computer Graphics: David Herman/Geoduck Graphics

ISBN 0-911019-34-0

Printed in the United States of America
Published by: Warren Publishing House, Inc.
                P.O. Box 2250
                Everett, WA 98203

20 19 18 17 16 15 14 13 12 11 10 9 8 7 6 5 4 3 2

CONTENTS

Introduction

Young children who are just becoming interested in books and reading are usually long on enthusiasm and short on ability. Totline "Take-Home" Books are designed to capture that enthusiasm.

Each of the pre-reading books in Animal Rhymes is about an animal or a group of animals and is written in rhyme. The unique feature of these rhymes is that young children are able to "read" them, using pictures as their guides. This happens because each rhyme is simply written and illustrated with pre-readers in mind. After reading a book with an adult a few times, your children will be able to "read" it by themselves.

Because all of the pre-reading books in this series are reproducible, your children can each have his or her own. And they will glow with pride and feelings of accomplishment as they take home their own books to "read" to their families.

General Directions

• Tear out the pages for the take-home book of your choice.

• Make one photocopy of the book for each child. Cut the pages in half.

• Place the pages on a table and let the children help collate them into books.

• Give each child two 5 1/2- by 8-inch pieces of construction paper to use for book covers.

• Let the children decorate their book covers as desired or use one of the suggestions on the following pages.

• Help the children bind their books using a stapler or a hole punch and brass paper fasteners.

Suggestions for Using the
Animal Rhymes
Take-Home Books

• The take-home books in *Animal Rhymes* are fun and easy to use. You can enlarge the pages to make big books for your room, introduce the rhymes with flannelboard cutouts or give out books at the end of a unit. Following are some ideas for using the take-home books with preschoolers, kindergartners and first and second graders. Mix and match the ideas to meet the needs and interests of your children.

Preschool

• Let the children use rubber stamps that correspond with the rhyme's subject to stamp the covers of their books.

• Give the children appropriate stickers to attach to the covers of their books.

• Make paint pads by folding paper towels, putting them in shallow containers and pouring small amounts of paint on them. Give the children animal cookie cutters to dip into the paint and then press on their book covers.

• Add extra pages to the end of each book. Cut out appropriate magazine pictures. Have the children glue them to their extra pages. Ask them to name or describe the pictures when they read their books.

• Ask the children to make the animals' sounds as they are named in the rhymes.

Kindergarten

• Have the children cut out and glue magazine pictures of the appropriate animals on their book covers.

• Have the children write their names on the backs of their books.

• Add extra lined pages to the back of each child's book. Have the children practice writing the names of the animals in the rhyme.

• Let the children act out the story as you read it aloud.

First and Second Grades

• Let the children take their books home to color.

• Have the children write "This book belongs to (child's name)" on their back covers.

• Have the children copy each sentence of a particular rhyme onto a separate page. Let them illustrate each of their pages.

• Photocopy each half page on a full sheet of paper with lines for writing below the picture. Have the children copy the words on the pages.

• Have the children cut out magazine pictures of the appropriate animals and glue them to the covers of their books.

• Let the children make up new stories about the animals in the rhymes. For example, "Monkey, monkey, in the zoo, who's that living next to you? Little alligator lives next door with her family of four." or "Who's that hiding under the mat? Did you guess? It's little cat."

Animals in the Zoo

Camel, camel in the zoo,

who's that living next to you?

Mother monkey lives next door

with her family of four.

Monkey, monkey in the zoo,

who's that living next to you?

Mother giraffe lives next door

with her family of four.

Giraffe, giraffe in the zoo,

who's that living next to you?

Mother elephant lives next door

with her family of four.

Elephant, elephant in the zoo,

who's that living next to you?

Mother hippopotamus lives next door

with her family of four.

Hippopotamus, hippopotamus in the zoo,

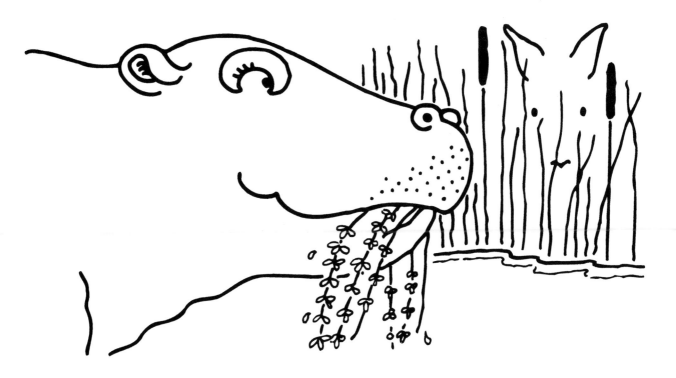

who's that living next to you?

Mother kangaroo lives next door

with her family of four.

Kangaroo, kangaroo in the zoo,

who's that living next to you?

Mother camel lives next door

with her family of four.

Animals in the Woods

Little owl, little owl, up in the tree.

Little owl, little owl, what do you see?

I see a bird up in the tree.

I see a bird looking at me.

Little bird, little bird, up in the tree.

Little bird, little bird, what do you see?

I see a squirrel up in the tree.

I see a squirrel looking at me.

Little squirrel, little squirrel, up in the tree.

Little squirrel, little squirrel, what do you see?

I see a bear up in the tree.

I see a bear looking at me.

Little bear, little bear, up in the tree.

Little bear, little bear, what do you see?

I see a raccoon up in the tree.

I see a raccoon looking at me.

Little raccoon, little raccoon, up in the tree.

Little raccoon, little raccoon, what do you see?

I see a porcupine up in the tree.

I see a porcupine looking at me.

Little porcupine, little porcupine, up in the tree.

Little porcupine, little porcupine, what do you see?

I see an owl up in the tree.

I see an owl looking at me.

Down on the Farm

Down on the farm early in the morning,

see the little ducks standing in a row.

See the busy farmer feeding them their breakfast.

Quack, quack, quack, quack, off they go.

Down on the farm early in the morning,

see the little pigs standing in a row.

See the busy farmer feeding them their breakfast.

Oink, oink, oink, oink, off they go.

Down on the farm early in the morning,

see the little cows standing in a row.

See the busy farmer feeding them their breakfast.

Moo, moo, moo, moo, off they go.

Down on the farm early in the morning,

see the little sheep standing in a row.

See the busy farmer feeding them their breakfast.

Baa, baa, baa, baa, off they go.

Down on the farm early in the morning,

see the little horses standing in a row.

See the busy farmer feeding them their breakfast.

Neigh, neigh, neigh, neigh, off they go.

Down on the farm early in the morning,

see the little chicks standing in a row.

See the busy farmer feeding them their breakfast.

Cheep, cheep, cheep, cheep, off they go.

In the
Blue Sea

I see a whale in the blue sea.

I see a whale swimming by me.

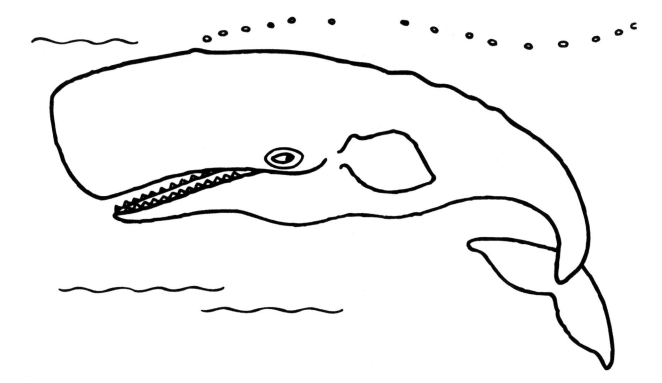

Little whale, little whale, in the blue sea.

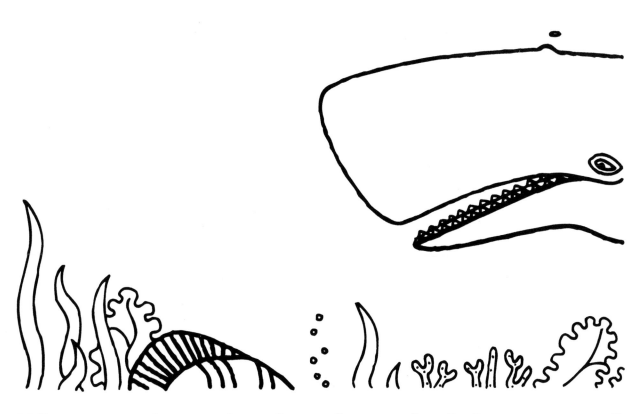

When you're out swimming, what do you see?

Little fish, little fish, in the blue sea.

When you're out swimming, what do you see?

I see a shark in the blue sea.

I see a shark swimming by me.

Little shark, little shark, in the blue sea.

When you're out swimming, what do you see?

I see an octopus in the blue sea.

I see an octopus swimming by me.

Little octopus, little octopus, in the blue sea.

When you're out swimming, what do you see?

I see a fish in the blue sea.

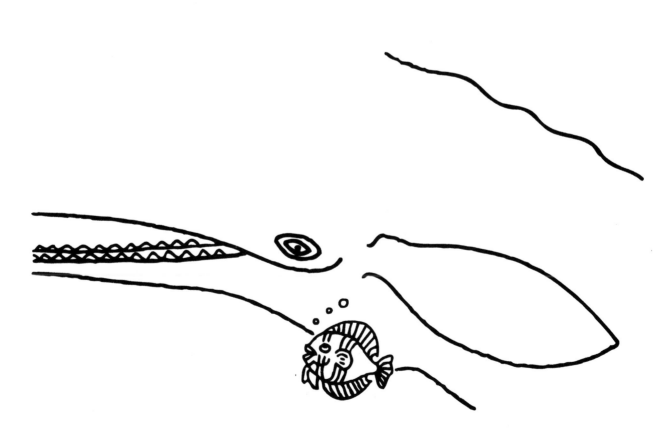

I see a fish swimming by me.

Who Is Hiding?

Who is hiding under the tree?

Did you guess? It's little bee.

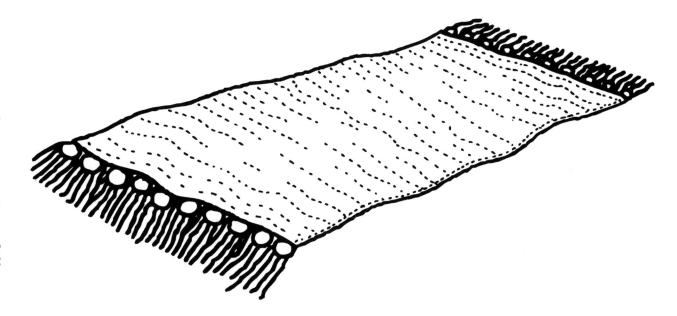

Who is hiding under the rug?

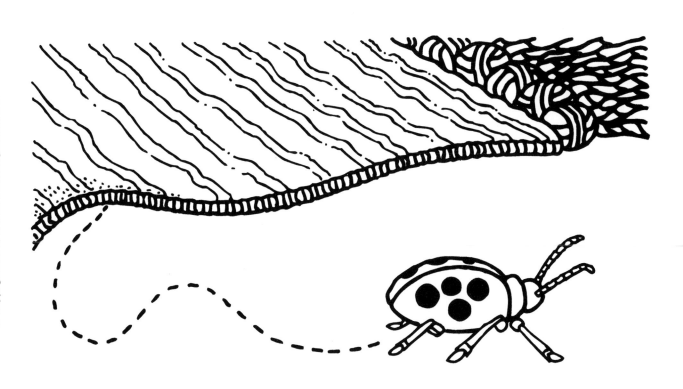

Did you guess? It's little bug.

Who is hiding under the house?

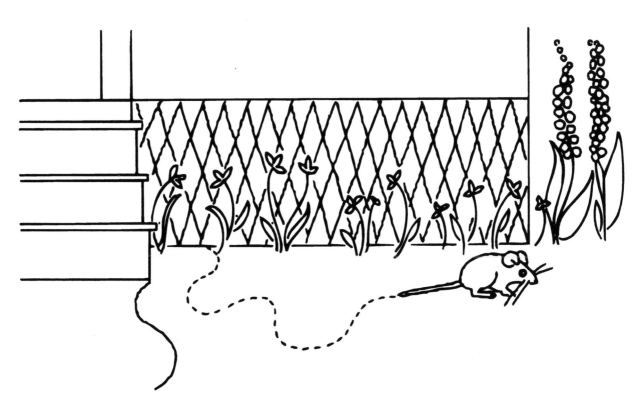

Did you guess? It's little mouse.

Who is hiding under the box?

Did you guess? It's little fox.

Who is hiding under the truck?

Did you guess? It's little duck.

Who is hiding under the hat?

Did you guess? It's little cat.

Who is hiding under the log?

Did you guess? It's little frog.

Monkey See, Monkey Do

Monkey, monkey, in the tree.

Can you jump around like me?

Monkey see, monkey do

Little monkey in the zoo.

Monkey, monkey, in the tree.

Can you twirl around like me?

Monkey see, monkey do

Little monkey in the zoo.

Monkey, monkey, in the tree.

Can you roll around like me?

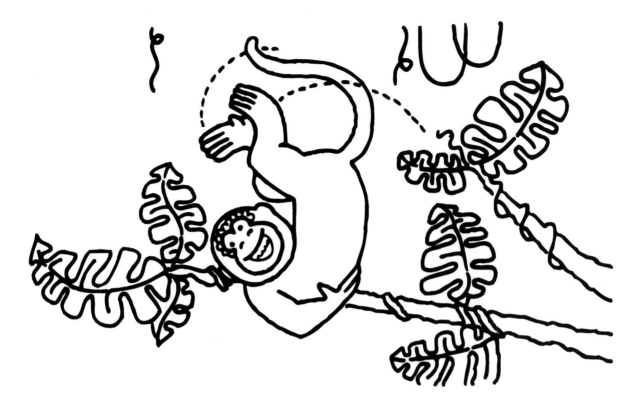

Monkey see, monkey do

Little monkey in the zoo.

Monkey, monkey, in the tree.

Can you dance around like me?

Monkey see, monkey do

Little monkey in the zoo.

Elephants in the Ring

One little elephant in the ring

walking on a piece of string.

My, my, what a stunt!

Let's all clap for the elephant.

Two little elephants in the ring

walking on a piece of string.

My, my, what a stunt!

Let's all clap for the elephant.

Three little elephants in the ring

walking on a piece of string.

My, my, what a stunt!

Let's all clap for the elephant.

Four little elephants in the ring

walking on a piece of string.

My, my, what a stunt!

Let's all clap for the elephant.

Five little elephants in the ring

walking on a piece of string.

My, my, what a stunt!

Let's all clap for the elephant.

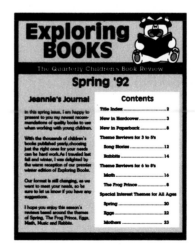

Totline® Books

Piggyback® Songs

More Piggyback® Songs

Piggyback® Songs
    for Infants and Toddlers

Piggyback® Songs
    in Praise of God

Piggyback® Songs
    in Praise of Jesus

Holiday Piggyback® Songs

Animal Piggyback® Songs

Piggyback® Songs for School

Piggyback® Sign to Sign

1·2·3 Art

1·2·3 Games

1·2·3 Colors

1·2·3 Puppets

1·2·3 Murals

1·2·3 Books

1·2·3 Reading & Writing

1·2·3 Rhymes, Stories & Songs

1·2·3· Math

Teeny-Tiny Folktales

Short-Short Stories

Mini-Mini Musicals

Small World Celebrations

Special Day Celebrations

Yankee Doodle
    Birthday Celebrations

Great Big Holiday Celebrations

"Cut & Tell"
    Scissor Stories for Fall

"Cut & Tell"
    Scissor Stories for Winter

"Cut & Tell"
    Scissor Stories for Spring

Alphabet Theme-A-Saurus®

Theme-A-Saurus®

Theme-A-Saurus® II

Toddler Theme-A-Saurus®

Alphabet & Number Rhymes

Color, Shape & Season Rhymes

Object Rhymes

Animal Rhymes

Our World

Our Selves

Animal Patterns

Everyday Patterns

Holiday Patterns

Nature Patterns

ABC Space

ABC Farm

ABC Zoo

ABC Circus

1001 Teaching Props

Super Snacks

Available at school supply stores and parent/teacher stores or write for our catalog.

Warren Publishing House, Inc. • P.O. Box 2250, Dept. B • Everett, WA 98203